French Activity Book

for ages 9-11

This CGP book has bags of fun activities
to build up children's knowledge and confidence.

There's even online audio for all the key words — perfect
for developing listening skills and pronunciation. Enjoy!

This book is a brilliant way to help children learn French vocabulary.

To access online audio of all the vocabulary in this book, head to cgpbooks.co.uk/primary-french-audio or scan this QR code on your smartphone.

Published by CGP

Editors:
Siân Butler, Hannah Roscoe, Hayley Shaw

With thanks to Keith Blackhall for the proofreading.

With thanks to Jade Sim for the copyright research.

ISBN: 978 1 83774 008 6

Printed by Zenith Print & Packaging Ltd, Pontypridd.
Clipart on the cover and throughout the book from Corel®
Cover design concept by emc design ltd.

Text, design, layout and original illustrations © Coordination Group Publications Ltd. (CGP) 2022
All rights reserved.

Photocopying this book is not permitted, even if you have a CLA licence.
Extra copies are available from CGP with next day delivery • 0800 1712 712 • www.cgpbooks.co.uk

Contents

Hello!	2
What is your name?	4
Numbers	6
Colours	8
Months	10
My family	12
Animals	14
Clothes	16
Puzzle: Magical masters	18
Food	20
What do you like doing?	22
What time is it?	24
The weather	26
In my town	28
Masculine and feminine	30
Plurals	32
Vocabulary	33
Answers	35

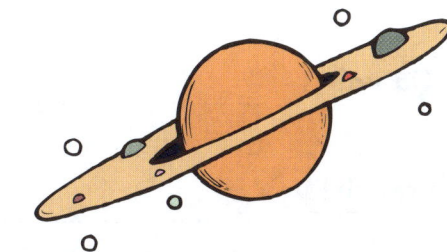

Hello!

How It Works

Here are some words and phrases you can use to greet someone in French:

bonsoir	good evening
bonne nuit	good night
à bientôt	see you soon

ça va bien	I'm well
bien	well
pas très bien	not very well

Now Try These

1. Unscramble these French phrases.

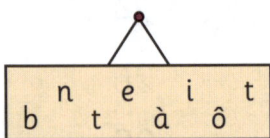
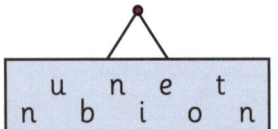
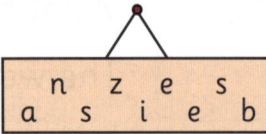

....

2. Write responses to complete the conversation below in French.

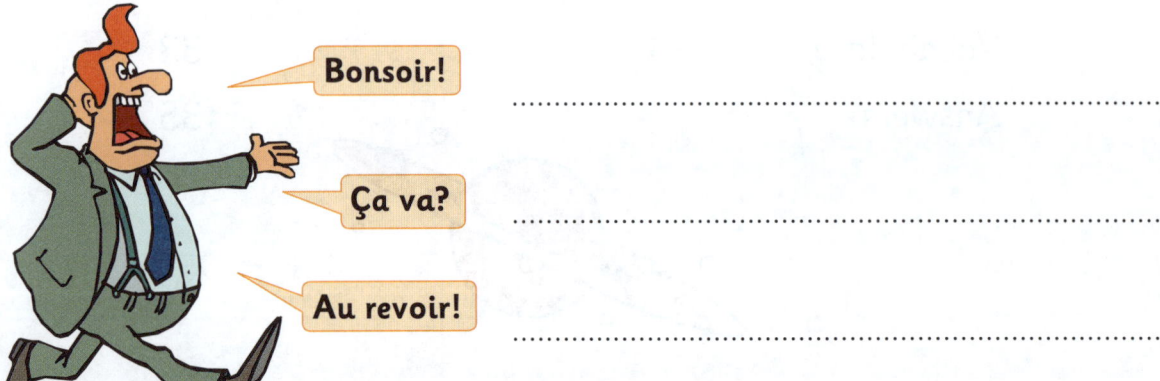

3. Read the speech bubbles and answer the questions below.

a) Who isn't feeling very well? ....
b) Who is feeling very well? ....
c) Who is feeling quite well? ....
d) Who is feeling well? ....
e) Who says 'see you soon' in French? ....
f) Who says 'good night' in French? ....

An Extra Challenge

Noémie is struggling to remember her conversation words in French. The English words below have all been hidden in the wordsearch in French. Can you help her by finding the French words?

good evening

thanks

well

hello

hi

Are you feeling fantastic after this section? Tick a box.

What is your name?

How It Works

To talk about people's names, you'll need these phrases:

Comment t'appelles-tu?
What is your name?

Je m'appelle Charlotte.
My name is Charlotte.

Il s'appelle Chompy.
He is called Chompy.

Elle s'appelle...
She is called...

Comment s'appellent-ils?
What are they called?

Ils s'appellent...
They are called...

Now Try These

1. Fill in the missing letters to complete the sentences below.

   Il ☐ ' a ☐ ☐ e ☐ ☐ Sam.

   Ils ☐ ' ☐ ☐ p ☐ l ☐ n ☐ Sanjay et Laura.

   Elle ☐ ' ☐ p ☐ ☐ ☐ ☐ e Lucie.

2. Write these sentences in English.

   a) Je m'appelle Deepti. ➔ ....

   b) Comment t'appelles-tu? ➔ ....

   c) Comment s'appellent-ils? ➔ ....

   d) Elle s'appelle Jane. ➔ ....

   e) Ils s'appellent Rosie et Joe. ➔ ....

3. Correct these sentences by crossing out the wrong words.

   a) Je m'appelle / ~~m'appelles~~ Zoe.
   b) Il s'appelle / s'appellent Alf.
   c) Il / Ils s'appelle David.
   d) Ils s'appelle / s'appellent Harry et Nicolas.
   e) Comment s'appelle / s'appellent -ils?.
   f) Comment t'appelle-tu / t'appelles-tu ?
   g) Ils / Elle s'appelle Leanne.

4. Write a sentence in French to introduce the people in each of these pictures.

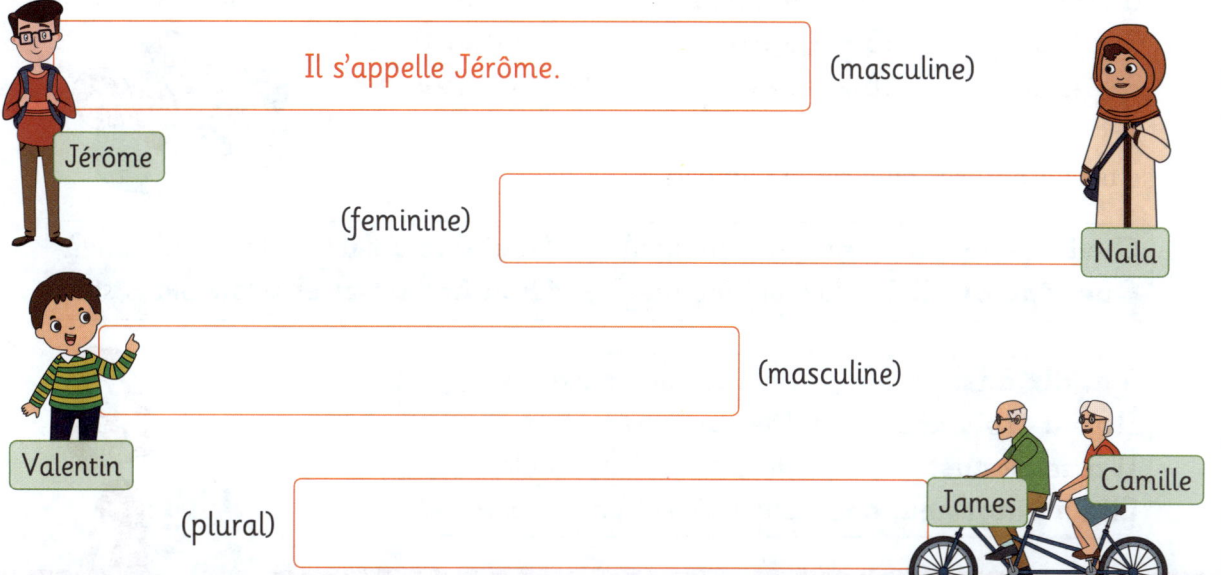

Jérôme — Il s'appelle Jérôme. (masculine)

Naila — (feminine)

Valentin — (masculine)

James & Camille — (plural)

An Extra Challenge

Class 6c have written letters introducing themselves to their French pen pals, but the words have got muddled up. Can you unscramble the words to make three sentences in French?

Word tiles: Marie, s', Alex, Jacob, m', appelle, Elle, Frankie, s', Je, appellent, et, appelle, Ils

Did you enjoy introducing yourself to these pages?

Numbers

How It Works

Here are the numbers from 1-30 in French:

les nombres numbers

1	un	9	neuf	17	dix-sept	25	vingt-cinq
2	deux	10	dix	18	dix-huit	26	vingt-six
3	trois	11	onze	19	dix-neuf	27	vingt-sept
4	quatre	12	douze	20	vingt	28	vingt-huit
5	cinq	13	treize	21	vingt-et-un	29	vingt-neuf
6	six	14	quatorze	22	vingt-deux	30	trente
7	sept	15	quinze	23	vingt-trois		
8	huit	16	seize	24	vingt-quatre		

These useful phrases all include numbers:

Quel âge as-tu?	How old are you?	**Quel âge a-t-il?**	How old is he?
Quel âge ont-ils?	How old are they?	**Quel âge a-t-elle?**	How old is she?

J'ai dix ans.	I am ten years old.
Ils ont trois ans.	They are three years old.
Il a seize ans.	He is sixteen years old.
Elle a vingt-neuf ans.	She is twenty-nine years old.

Now Try These

1. Count how many items there are in each group. Write the number in French in the box.

a)

dix-neuf

c)

b)

d)

2. Write the answers to these sums in French.

   a) onze + douze = vingt-trois   d) vingt-quatre − sept =

   b) seize + cinq =   e) vingt-huit − dix =

   c) trente − quinze =   f) dix-sept + huit =

3. Match each question with a suitable answer and write the age in the box.

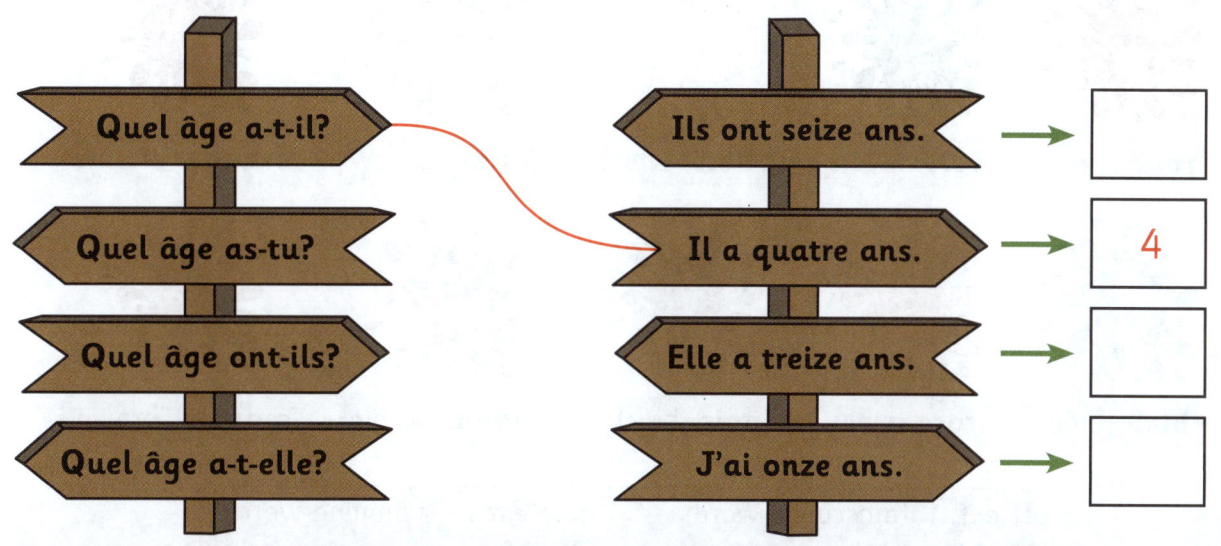

Quel âge a-t-il?	Ils ont seize ans.	
Quel âge as-tu?	Il a quatre ans.	4
Quel âge ont-ils?	Elle a treize ans.	
Quel âge a-t-elle?	J'ai onze ans.	

An Extra Challenge

Henri, Maisam and Sita have had their birthdays this month. Can you write a sentence to say how old each person is in French? You need to write the numbers in **words**.

 Henri

 Maisam

 Sita

....

....

....

Have these pages added to your French knowledge? Tick a box.

Colours

How It Works

Read the words and phrases, then answer the questions below.

les couleurs colours

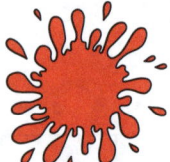 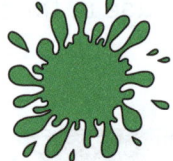   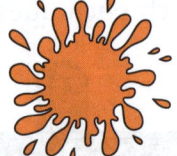

rouge red   **vert** green   **blanc** white   **jaune** yellow   **orange** orange

 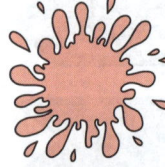  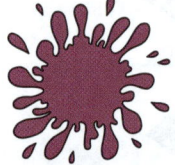 

bleu blue   **rose** pink   **noir** black   **violet** purple   **marron** brown

Il est... (masculine words)   **Elle est...** (feminine words)
He / It is...   She / It is...

Now Try These

1. Write the correct colour in French on each label.

2. Unscramble the letters to spell the colours in French. Write the English words next to them.

a) i o r n
noir — black

b) t e v r
....

c) l e u b
....

d) l c a n b
....

e) o r e u g
....

f) u e a n j
....

An Extra Challenge

Can you write a sentence in each box to describe what colour the items are? You'll need to use 'Il' or 'Elle'.

Remember! In French, there are two words for 'the'. 'Le' is used for masculine words and 'la' is used for feminine words.

Il est jaune.

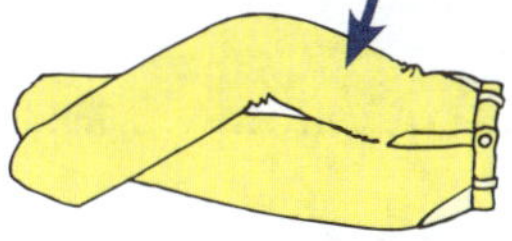

le pantalon

le chapeau

le chien

la vache

la fleur

Did you pass this page with flying colours? Tick a box.

Months

How It Works

Here are the words you'll need to talk about the months in French:

les mois	months
janvier	January
février	February
mars	March
avril	April
mai	May
juin	June
juillet	July
août	August
septembre	September
octobre	October
novembre	November
décembre	December

Quelle est la date de ton anniversaire?
When is your birthday?

C'est le dix mai.
It's the 10th of May.

Remember! In French, the first letters of months are lower case.

Now Try These

1. Answer the questions below in French.

    a) Which month comes after **mars**? ....

    b) Which month comes three months after **juin**? ....

    c) Which month comes before **janvier**? ....

    d) Which month comes before **août**? ....

2. In French, write when each chef's birthday is.

C'est le six mai.
6th May

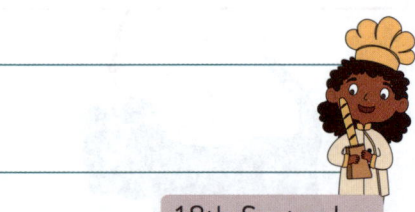
18th September

2nd June

26th February

3. Write these sentences in English.

   a) C'est le vingt-trois mars.   It's the 23rd of March.

   b) C'est le trente novembre.   ....

   c) C'est le douze juillet.   ....

   d) C'est le quatre août.   ....

   e) C'est le premier avril.   ....

4. Answer the question below, in French.

Quelle est la date de ton anniversaire?

Remember!
If the date is the first of the month you say 'le premier', e.g. 'C'est le premier août', which means 'It's the first of August'.

An Extra Challenge

Katrina has dropped her calendar and now the pages are mixed up. Can you help her get everything in order again by finding the French months of the year in the wordsearch?

~~January~~
February
March
April
May
June
July
August
September
October
November
December

o	s	e	p	t	e	m	b	r	e	b	a
c	e	d	h	d	é	c	e	m	b	r	e
t	û	a	w	j	c	i	s	t	f	n	g
o	p	o	m	u	l	é	l	b	i	o	f
b	é	û	c	i	d	e	m	a	i	v	é
r	d	t	g	n	a	e	a	a	j	e	v
e	c	f	a	j	h	b	r	û	d	m	r
e	a	v	r	i	l	d	s	k	s	b	i
é	b	k	j	u	i	l	l	e	t	r	e
j	a	n	v	i	e	r	n	s	o	e	r

Are you marvellous at talking about months? Tick a box.

My family

How It Works

To talk about your family in French, you'll need these words:

- **ma famille** — my family
- **ma mère** — my mother
- **mon père** — my father
- **mon grand-père** — my grandfather
- **ma grand-mère** — my grandmother
- **moi** — me
- **ma sœur** — my sister
- **mon frère** — my brother
- **mon beau-père** — my stepfather
- **ma belle-mère** — my stepmother

Remember! The word for 'my' changes. If the following word is feminine, use 'ma', and if the word is masculine, use 'mon'.

Tu as des frères ou des sœurs?
Do you have any brothers or sisters?

Oui, j'ai un frère et une sœur.
Yes, I have one brother and a sister.

Non, je suis fils unique.
No, I'm an only child *(boy)*.

Non, je suis fille unique.
No, I'm an only child *(girl)*.

Now Try These

1. Write these sentences in French.

    a) Do you have any brothers or sisters?

    ....

    ....

    b) Yes, I have two sisters and a brother.

    ....

    ....

    c) My name is Adam and I'm an only child.

    ....

    ....

Remember! If you're talking about more than one brother or sister add an 's', e.g. 'deux frères'.

2. Read the text and answer the questions in English.

> Ma mère s'appelle Belinda et mon père s'appelle Geoffrey. Mon beau-père s'appelle Lloyd et ma grand-mère s'appelle Rita. Ma sœur s'appelle Emily et elle a quinze ans. Mon frère s'appelle Lucas et il a vingt ans.

a) What is Élodie's mother called? ..... Belinda .....

b) How old is Élodie's brother? ....

c) Who is Lloyd? ....

d) How old is Élodie's sister? ....

e) What is Élodie's father called? ....

f) Who is Rita? ....

g) What is Élodie's sister called? ....

An Extra Challenge

Ronan's dad is showing him their family tree. Can you use the picture to complete what Ronan has written about his family? Then write about your own family.

Je m'appelle Ronan. J'ai un .... qui s'appelle Jaxon. .... s'appelle Maya et .... s'appelle Hamed. .... s'appelle Derek et .... s'appelle Pauline.

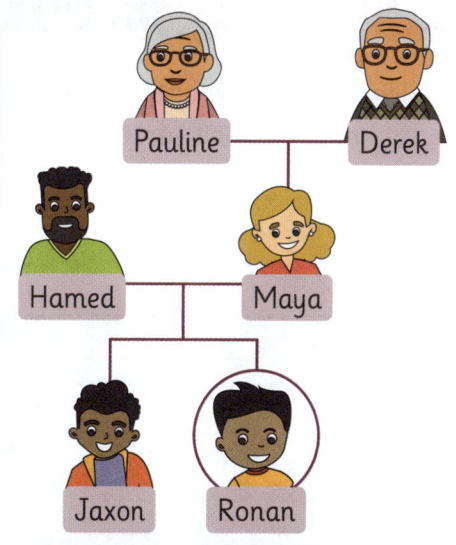

Do you feel fabulous about family vocabulary? Tick a box.

Animals

How It Works

Here are some words and phrases to help you talk about animals in French.

 les animaux — animals

le chien dog   **le cheval** horse   **le lapin** rabbit   **l'oiseau** bird   **la souris** mouse   **le chat** cat

le hamster hamster   **le poisson** fish   **le serpent** snake   **l'araignée** spider   **la tortue** tortoise

Remember!

L'oiseau is a masculine word and *l'araignée* is feminine. When words begin with a vowel, the 'le' or 'la' becomes 'l''.

As-tu un animal? — Do you have a pet?
Oui, j'ai... — Yes, I have...
Non, je n'ai pas d'animaux. — No, I don't have any pets.

Now Try These

1. Unscramble the letters to spell the names of some animals in French. Don't forget to include either 'la', 'le' or 'l''.

   a) é a a l' g e n r i → ....

   b) i e h c e l n → ....

   c) s n o i p s e l o → ....

   d) s l e e t r e n p → ....

2. Write the correct French word for each picture below.

a)

b)

c)

d)

3. Read the text and answer the questions in English.

> J'ai trois chiens et un chat. Mon chat s'appelle Scruffy et il a deux ans. J'ai quatre lapins et trois araignées.

Claude

a) How many dogs does Claude have? ....

b) Claude owns six spiders. True or false? ....

c) Who is Scruffy? ....

d) How old is Scruffy? ....

e) Claude has four of what animal? ....

An Extra Challenge

Your French pen pal, Mathilde, has sent you an email asking 'As-tu un animal?'. Can you write a response in French on the lines below? Give details about your animals.

Email

To: mathilde@abcdmail.net

Subject: Les animaux

....
....
....

Did you fly through this animal vocabulary? Tick a box.

Clothes

How It Works

Read these words and phrases about clothes, then answer the questions below.

les vêtements clothes

le jean	jeans	les chaussettes	socks
la chemise	shirt	les chaussures	shoes
le pantalon	trousers	la robe	dress
le pull	jumper	le chapeau	hat
la jupe	skirt	les gants	gloves
le t-shirt	T-shirt		

Remember! In French, the words 'le', 'la' and 'les' all mean 'the'. If you want to say 'a', e.g. 'a dress', you should change 'le' to 'un' and 'la' to 'une'. 'les' changes to 'des', which means 'some'.

Je porte...	I am wearing...
Il porte...	He is wearing...
Elle porte...	She is wearing...

Now Try These

1. Write the English next to each French word.

   a) le pantalon ....   d) la jupe ....

   b) les gants ....   e) la robe ....

   c) la chemise ....   f) le jean ....

2. Write a sentence in French to say what these characters are wearing.

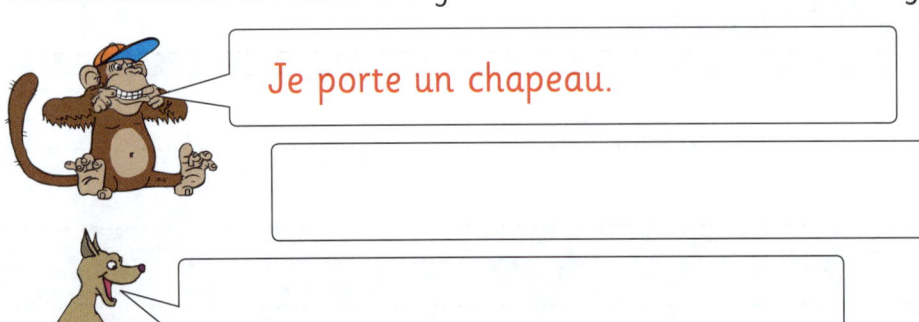

Je porte un chapeau.

3. Circle the sentence that describes each picture best.

Remember!
In French, describing words like 'bleu' come after the noun, e.g. 'un jean bleu'.

~~Il porte un t-shirt bleu.~~ (circled)

Il porte un pull noir.

Il porte un pantalon blanc.

Il porte des chaussures vertes.

Il porte un pantalon rouge.

Il porte un t-shirt blanc.

Elle porte une jupe rose.

Elle porte un chapeau violet.

Elle porte une chemise verte.

Elle porte un pull jaune.

Elle porte une robe orange.

Elle porte un pantalon marron.

An Extra Challenge

You meet Niklaus while you're on holiday in France. Can you use what he says to help you answer the questions below? Give your answers in English.

> Je porte un chapeau vert, une chemise jaune et un pantalon noir.
> Mon frère s'appelle Florian. Il porte un pull marron et un jean bleu.
> Ma sœur s'appelle Kalena. Elle porte une jupe rouge et un t-shirt violet.

Niklaus

a) Who is wearing a brown jumper? ....

b) What colour are Niklaus's trousers? ....

c) Who is wearing a purple T-shirt? ....

d) Who is wearing blue jeans? ....

e) What colour is Kalena's skirt? ....

Are you dressed to impress for French success? Tick a box.

Magical masters

Wizards from across the magical realms are gathering in Calandel for the annual talent show. Bertha the Brilliant wants to wow the judges with her amazing skills. Can you help her triumph?

1. Bertha is preparing to go to Calandel. She has a weather forecast for the day she plans to travel. Read what the forecast says, then help Bertha fill in the missing symbols on the map.

City of Calandel
Il fait beau. Il y a du soleil.

Fairy Forest
Il y a du vent et il fait froid.

Stinky Swamp
Il pleut et il fait chaud.

Misty Mountains
Il fait mauvais. Il neige.

Rumbling River
Il y a du soleil et il y a du vent.

2. The first event of the talent show is the Transformation Test, where wizards have to turn themselves into an animal. They score points for different transformations, and whoever gets the most points is the winner. Use the scoresheet to work out how many points each transformation scores, then circle the animal that Bertha should become to win.

Scoresheet
trois — oiseau, chat, araignée
cinq — chien, cheval, tortue
sept — poisson, hamster, lapin
dix — blanc, noir, marron
douze — rouge, vert, jaune
quinze — bleu, orange, violet

3. a) Bertha is completing a potions challenge. She casts a spell on each potion to reveal its secret ingredient. Help Bertha by writing the names of the ingredients in French on the list below.

Secret Ingredient List
(Don't forget the 'le', 'la' or 'l'')

-
-
-
-
-

b) To activate each potion, Bertha needs to circle the ingredients that are masculine and underline the ones that are feminine. Can you help her?

4. Bertha has been nominated for the Most Magnificent Mage award. The judges want to know more about the finalists, so she needs to write a speech about what she enjoys doing. Can you help her write what she wants to say in French?

I like playing football. I like listening to music at six o'clock in the evening. I don't like watching TV. I like reading because it's interesting. I don't like playing the piano because it's boring.

19

Food

How It Works

Read these words and phrases you'll need to talk about food in French.

la nourriture food

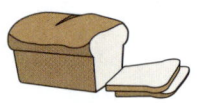
le pain bread

les frites chips

le sandwich sandwich

le jambon ham

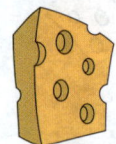
le fromage cheese

la pomme apple

le chocolat chocolate

la pizza pizza

les spaghettis spaghetti

le yaourt yoghurt

la fourchette	the fork
le couteau	the knife
la cuillère	the spoon
l'assiette	the plate

Peux-tu me passer le couteau s'il te plaît?
Can you pass me the knife, please?

Remember!
In French, the words 'le', 'la' and 'les' all mean 'the'. If you want to say 'some' instead, you should change 'le' to 'du', 'la' to 'de la' and 'les' to 'des', e.g. 'Je mange du pain' — 'I am eating some bread'.

Je mange... I'm eating...

Je voudrais... I would like...

Now Try These

1. Draw lines to match the pictures to the French words.

 l'assiette

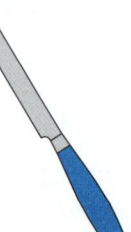 le couteau

la fourchette

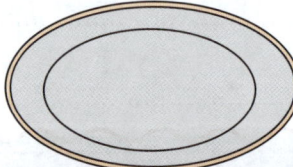

la cuillère

2. Unscramble these French words.

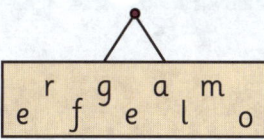 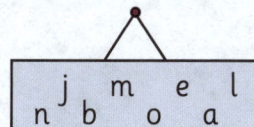 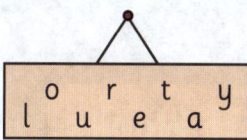

....

3. Write these sentences in English.

   a) Peux-tu me passer la fourchette, s'il te plaît?

   ....

   b) Je mange du chocolat.

   ....

   c) Peux-tu me passer la cuillère?

   ....

   d) Je voudrais une assiette.

   ....

An Extra Challenge

Rowena and Gabe are looking for items in the supermarket. Can you write the right name next to each bag of food? Then write your own shopping list.

Je voudrais quatre yaourts, le fromage et du pain.

Rowena

Je voudrais un sandwich, trois pommes et du jambon.

Gabe

....

....

Are you full of food vocabulary? Put a tick in one of the boxes.

What do you like doing?

How It Works

To talk to people about hobbies, you can use these phrases:

Qu'est-ce que tu aimes faire?
What do you like doing?

J'aime...
I like...

Je n'aime pas...
I don't like...

...jouer au foot
...playing football

...danser
...dancing

...nager
...swimming

...jouer du piano
...playing the piano

...regarder la télé
...watching TV

...écouter de la musique
...listening to music

...lire
...reading

Pourquoi?
Why?

C'est fantastique.
It's fantastic.

C'est nul.
It's rubbish.

Parce que...
Because...

C'est intéressant.
It's interesting.

C'est ennuyeux.
It's boring.

Now Try These

1. Write these sentences in English.

   J'aime regarder la télé. → ....

   .... ← Je n'aime pas danser.

   J'aime jouer au foot. → ....

2. In French, write what each person likes or dislikes doing.

 ....Je n'aime pas lire..

....

 ....

....

3. Read the letter and answer the questions in English.

   a) Name two things that Agnès likes doing.

   ....

   b) What does Agnès say is fantastic?

   ....

   c) What does Agnès say is boring?

   ....

   d) What does Agnès say is rubbish?

   ....

   e) What does Agnès say is interesting?

   ....

> J'aime lire, parce que c'est intéressant. J'aime jouer au foot, parce que c'est fantastique. Je n'aime pas regarder la télé, parce que c'est nul. Je n'aime pas danser, parce que c'est ennuyeux.
>
> Agnès

An Extra Challenge

At the end of Agnès's letter, she asks 'Qu'est-ce que tu aimes faire? Pourquoi?'. Can you write a response to her on the lines below?

Bonjour Agnès,

....

....

....

....

....

Is French one of your hobbies? Tick a box to show how you did.

What time is it?

How It Works

To talk about the time in French, you'll need these phrases.

Quelle heure est-il?
What time is it?

Il est deux heures...
It's two o'clock...

À dix heures...
At ten o'clock...

...du matin
...in the morning

...du soir
...in the evening

Il est dix heures et quart.
It's quarter past ten.

Il est dix heures et demie.
It's half past ten.

Il est midi.
It's midday.

Il est minuit.
It's midnight.

Now Try These

1. Draw the hands on the clocks to show the correct times.

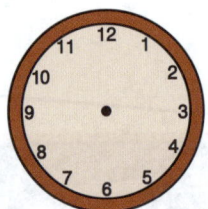
Il est huit heures et quart.

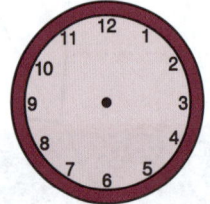
Il est onze heures et demie.

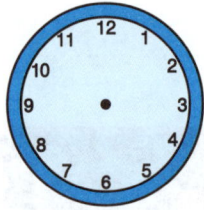
Il est minuit.

Il est trois heures et demie.

2. Monique has written down what she likes doing on a Saturday. Answer the questions about her routine in English.

   a) When does Monique like to dance?
      ...2 o'clock...

   b) What does Monique like to do at 11 am?
      ....

   c) When does Monique like to play the piano?
      ....

   d) What does Monique like to do at 8 pm?
      ....

> À dix heures du matin, je joue au foot.
>
> À onze heures du matin, je regarde la télé.
>
> À deux heures, je danse.
>
> À six heures du soir, je joue du piano.
>
> À huit heures du soir, j'écoute de la musique.

3. Look at the clock, then write down what time it is in French.

   ...... Il est une heure. ......

   ....

   ....

4. Read the question below and give your answer in French.

   Quelle heure est-il?

An Extra Challenge

Jakub and Adjoa are talking about when they do their hobbies. Can you rewrite what they both say in French? Then, write a sentence about when you do your own hobbies in French.

Remember! In French, words like 'nager' can mean 'to swim' as well as 'swimming'.

At three o'clock, I like to play football.

....

....

At quarter past six in the evening, I like to dance.

....

....

Are you terrific at telling the time? Put a tick in a box.

The weather

How It Works

Here are some phrases you can use to talk about the weather in French.

| le temps | Il fait... | ...beau. | ...good weather. | ...froid. | ...cold. |
| the weather | It is... | ...mauvais. | ...bad weather. | ...chaud. | ...hot. |

Il y a du soleil. It is sunny.   Il neige. It is snowing.   Il pleut. It is raining.
Il y a du vent. It is windy.

Quel temps fait-il (aujourd'hui)?
What's the weather like (today)?

Now Try These

1. Match each French phrase to the correct English phrase.

   Il fait beau.   It's cold.   It's hot.   Il fait froid.

   It's bad weather.   Il neige.   It's nice weather.

   Il fait chaud.   It's snowing.   Il fait mauvais.

2. Fill in the blanks below to form sentences in French.

_ _ _ _ _ _ _ _ _ _ .

_ _ _ _ _ _ _ _ _ _ _ _ .

_ _ _ _ _ _ _ _ .

_ _ _ _ _ _ _ _ .

3. Read the question below and give your answer in French.

Quel temps fait-il aujourd'hui?

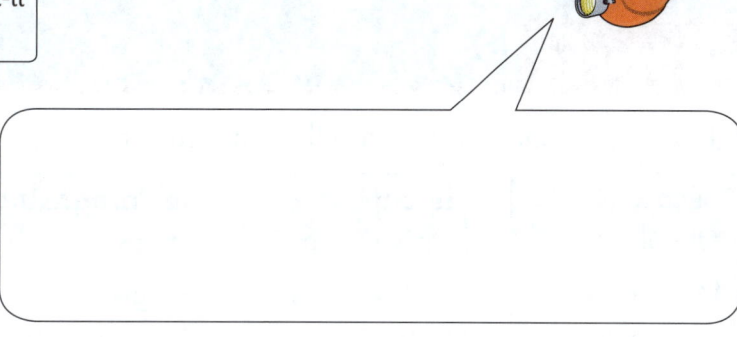

4. Write these sentences in French.

a) It is bad weather. ....

b) It is cold. ....

c) It is hot. ....

An Extra Challenge

Tara tried to keep a weather diary while she was on holiday in France, but she was so busy that she forgot to fill in some of the information. Can you use the pictures and sentences to help her complete the diary?

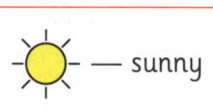 — sunny
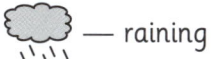 — raining
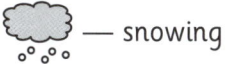 — snowing
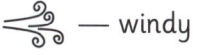 — windy
 — hot
 — cold

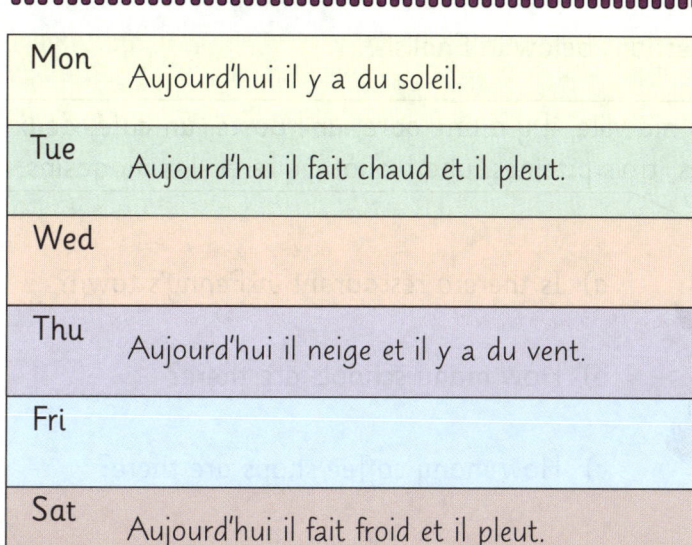

Day	Sentence	Picture
Mon	Aujourd'hui il y a du soleil.	☀
Tue	Aujourd'hui il fait chaud et il pleut.	
Wed		☀
Thu	Aujourd'hui il neige et il y a du vent.	
Fri		❄
Sat	Aujourd'hui il fait froid et il pleut.	

Do you love French come rain or shine? Put a tick in a box.

In my town

How It Works

Use these words and phrases to talk about your town.

l'école school	**le café** coffee shop	**les magasins** shops	**la bibliothèque** library
la piscine swimming pool	**le restaurant** restaurant	**la gare** train station	**la poste** post office

Dans ma ville, il y a… In my town, there is / are…

Où est…? Where is…?	**à côté de…** next to…	**près de…** near to…	**en face de…** opposite…

Now Try These

1. Unscramble these French phrases.

   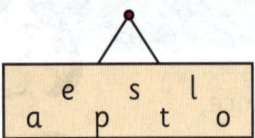   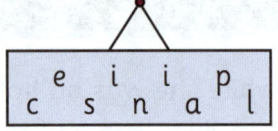   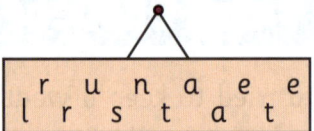

   …… ………………………………   …… ………………………………   …… ………………………………

2. Answer the questions below in English.

   Remember! 'Il y a' means 'there is' or 'there are'.

   Dans ma ville, il y a une gare, une poste, un café, deux écoles, trois piscines, une bibliothèque et des magasins.

   a) Is there a restaurant in Penny's town? …………………………………

   b) How many schools are there? …………………………………

   c) How many coffee shops are there? …………………………………

   d) How many swimming pools are there? …………………………………

   e) Is there a library in Penny's town? …………………………………

3. Answer the questions below in English.

La piscine est à côté de la poste. La gare est en face de la poste et près du café.

Le café est à côté de la gare et en face de l'école. La bibliothèque est en face du restaurant.

Remember!
In French, 'de le' becomes 'du'. So you say 'en face du restaurant', not 'en face de le restaurant'.

a) Où est la gare?

Opposite the post office / near the coffee shop.

b) Où est la bibliothèque?

c) Où est la piscine?

An Extra Challenge

Your French cousin, Raphaël, has sent you an email asking about what is in your town. Can you write a response in French on the lines below? Give details about where you can find the different places.

Email

To: raphaël@abcdmail.net

Subject: Ma ville

Did you navigate these pages well? Put a tick in a box.

Masculine and feminine

How It Works

All objects in French are either masculine or feminine. This means that the French words for 'the', 'a' and 'my' change depending on whether the word that follows is masculine or feminine.

feminine
la chemise — the shirt
une chemise — a shirt
ma chemise — my shirt

masculine
le pull — the jumper
un pull — a jumper
mon pull — my jumper

Now Try These

1. Fill in the gaps below with either 'mon' or 'ma'.

Remember! If you're unsure whether a word is masculine or feminine, look back through this book.

a) ...Mon... pull est vert.   .... pull est violet.

b) .... jupe est rose.   .... t-shirt est jaune.

c) .... chien est marron et blanc. .... chat est orange et violet.

d) .... chapeau est bleu et .... chemise est verte.

2. Write the French words for the items below on the correct clipboard.

masculine

le jambon

feminine

3. Fill in the gaps below with either 'un' or 'une'.

Je porte .... chapeau orange et .... chemise rose.

J'ai .... frère et .... sœur.

Je mange .... pomme, ... yaourt et .... sandwich.

An Extra Challenge

Casper is confused about how to use masculine and feminine. Can you help him by using the words below to complete the passage? Then, write some sentences of your own. Make sure to pay attention to whether the objects are masculine or feminine.

| la | la | un | une | mon | ma |

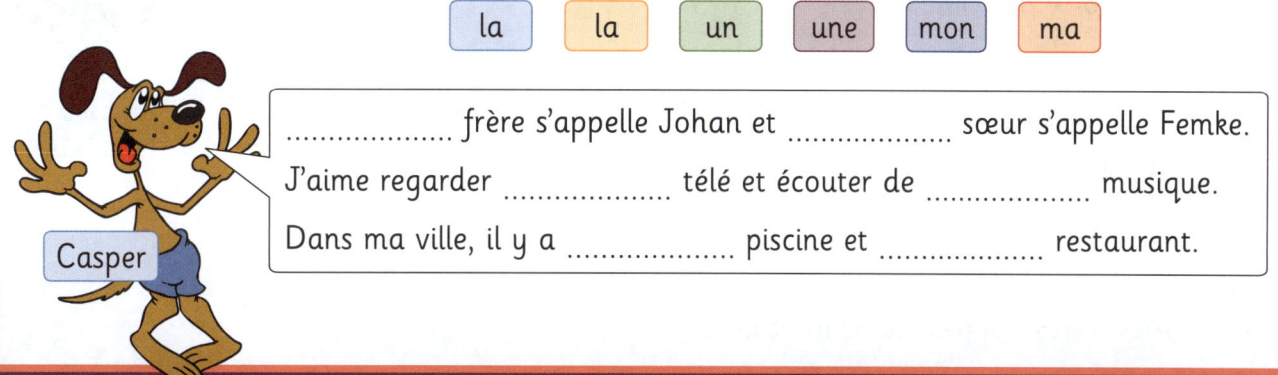

Casper

.... frère s'appelle Johan et .... sœur s'appelle Femke.
J'aime regarder .... télé et écouter de .... musique.
Dans ma ville, il y a .... piscine et .... restaurant.

Have you mastered masculine and feminine? Tick a box.

31

Plurals

How It Works

If there's more than one of something, you need to add an 's' to the end of the word (unless there already is an 's').

une pomme	deux pommes	une souris	deux souris
one apple	two apples	one mouse	two mice

masculine
le chat — the cat
les chats — the cats
mes chats — my cats
des chats — some cats

feminine
la jupe — the skirt
les jupes — the skirts
mes jupes — my skirts
des jupes — some skirts

Now Try These

1. Write the following phrases in French.

   a) the sisters ..... *les sœurs* .....

   b) my hamsters ....

   c) some apples ....

   d) the shops ....

   e) some dresses ....

   f) my snakes ....

   g) the T-shirts ....

   h) my jumpers ....

2. Write these sentences in English.

   a) Elle porte des chaussures.

   ....

   b) Je mange des frites.

   ....

   c) Mes frères s'appellent Henri et Léo.

   ....

Je mange des chaussures.

Vocabulary

Hello! — Bonjour!

salut	hi	très bien	very well
au revoir	goodbye	ça va bien	I'm well
bonsoir	good evening	bien	well
bonne nuit	good night	assez bien	quite well
à bientôt	see you soon	pas très bien	not very well
Ça va?	How are you?		

What is your name? — Comment t'appelles-tu?

Je m'appelle...	I am called...	Comment s'appellent-ils?	What are they called?
Il s'appelle...	He is called...	Ils s'appellent...	They are called...
Elle s'appelle...	She is called...		

Numbers — Les nombres

un	1	neuf	9	dix-sept	17	vingt-cinq	25
deux	2	dix	10	dix-huit	18	vingt-six	26
trois	3	onze	11	dix-neuf	19	vingt-sept	27
quatre	4	douze	12	vingt	20	vingt-huit	28
cinq	5	treize	13	vingt-et-un	21	vingt-neuf	29
six	6	quatorze	14	vingt-deux	22	trente	30
sept	7	quinze	15	vingt-trois	23		
huit	8	seize	16	vingt-quatre	24		

Colours — Les couleurs

rouge	red	blanc	white	noir	black
vert	green	orange	orange	marron	brown
bleu	blue	rose	pink	Il est...	He / It is...
jaune	yellow	violet	purple	Elle est...	She / It is...

Months — Les mois

janvier	January	septembre	September
février	February	octobre	October
mars	March	novembre	November
avril	April	décembre	December
mai	May	Quelle est la date de ton anniversaire?	When is your birthday?
juin	June		
juillet	July	C'est le dix mai.	It's the 10th of May.
août	August		

My family — Ma famille

moi	me	mon beau-père	my stepfather
ma mère	my mother	ma belle-mère	my stepmother
mon père	my father	Tu as des frères ou des sœurs?	Do you have any brothers or sisters?
mon frère	my brother		
ma sœur	my sister	Oui, j'ai un frère et une sœur.	Yes, I have a brother and a sister.
ma grand-mère	my grandmother	Je suis fils unique.	I am an only child. *(boy)*
mon grand-père	my grandfather	Je suis fille unique.	I am an only child. *(girl)*

Vocabulary

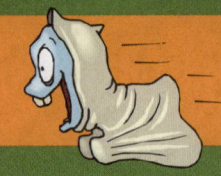

Animals — Les animaux

le chien	dog	le chat	cat	la tortue	tortoise
le cheval	horse	le hamster	hamster	As-tu un animal?	Do you have a pet?
le lapin	rabbit	le poisson	fish	Oui, j'ai...	Yes, I have...
l'oiseau	bird	le serpent	snake	Non, je n'ai pas d'animaux.	No, I don't have any pets.
la souris	mouse	l'araignée	spider		

Clothes — Les vêtements

le jean	jeans	le t-shirt	T-shirt	les gants	gloves
la chemise	shirt	les chaussettes	socks	Je porte...	I am wearing...
le pantalon	trousers	les chaussures	shoes	Il porte...	He is wearing...
le pull	jumper	la robe	dress	Elle porte...	She is wearing...
la jupe	skirt	le chapeau	hat		

Food — La nourriture

le pain	bread	le chocolat	chocolate	la fourchette	the fork
les frites	chips	la pizza	pizza	le couteau	the knife
le sandwich	sandwich	les spaghettis	spaghetti	la cuillère	the spoon
le jambon	ham	le yaourt	yoghurt	l'assiette	the plate
le fromage	cheese	Je mange...	I am eating...		
la pomme	apple	Je voudrais...	I would like...		

What do you like doing? — Qu'est-ce que tu aimes faire?

J'aime...	I like...	jouer du piano	playing the piano
Je n'aime pas...	I don't like...	regarder la télé	watching television
lire	reading	écouter de la musique	listening to music
danser	dancing	jouer au foot	playing football
nager	swimming	Pourquoi? Parce que...	Why? Because...

What time is it? — Quelle heure est-il?

Il est deux heures.	It's two o'clock.	Il est dix heures et quart.	It's quarter past ten.
À dix heures...	At ten o'clock...	Il est dix heures et demie.	It's half past ten.
du matin	in the morning	Il est midi.	It's midday.
du soir	in the evening	Il est minuit.	It's midnight.

The weather — Le temps

Il fait beau.	It is nice weather.	Il y a du vent.	It is windy.
Il fait mauvais.	It is bad weather.	Il neige.	It is snowing.
Il fait froid.	It is cold.	Il pleut.	It is raining.
Il fait chaud.	It is hot.	Quel temps fait-il (aujourd'hui)?	What's the weather like (today)?
Il y a du soleil.	It is sunny.		

In my town — Dans ma ville

l'école	school	la gare	train station	à côté de...	next to...
la piscine	swimming pool	la bibliothèque	library	près de...	near to...
le café	coffee shop	la poste	post office	en face de...	opposite...
le restaurant	restaurant	Il y a...	There is / are...		
les magasins	shops	Où est...?	Where is...?		

Answers

Pages 2-3 — Hello!

1. à bientôt
   bonne nuit
   assez bien

2. Any sensible answers, e.g.
   Bonsoir.
   Très bien, merci.
   À bientôt!

3. a) Amy
   b) Beth
   c) Paul
   d) Anna
   e) Amy
   f) Paul

   An Extra Challenge

   ```
   b  o  n  s  o  i  r  v  g
   o  t  d  i  j  w  i  b  h
   n  g  s  n  a  q  c  o  u
   j  l  f  j  o  m  r  n  l
   o  l  x  m  t  e  e  j  a
   u  c  v  u  e  r  m  y  s
   r  i  l  u  r  c  x  p  k
   m  a  j  h  d  b  i  e  n
   s  b  u  k  f  z  u  i  e
   ```

Pages 4-5 — What is your name?

1. Il s'appelle Sam.
   Ils s'appellent Sanjay et Laura.
   Elle s'appelle Lucie.

2. a) My name is Deepti.
   b) What is your name?
   c) What are they called?
   d) She is called Jane.
   e) They are called Rosie and Joe.

3. b) Il <u>s'appelle</u> Alf.
   c) <u>Il</u> s'appelle David.
   d) Ils <u>s'appellent</u> Harry et Nicolas.
   e) Comment <u>s'appellent</u>-ils?
   f) Comment <u>t'appelles</u>-tu?
   g) <u>Elle</u> s'appelle Leanne.

4. Elle s'appelle Naila.
   Il s'appelle Valentin.
   Ils s'appellent James et Camille.

An Extra Challenge
Any sensible sentences, e.g.
Je m'appelle Marie.
Ils s'appellent Frankie et Jacob.
Elle s'appelle Alex.

Pages 6-7 — Numbers

1. b) douze
   c) seize
   d) vingt-six

2. b) seize + cinq = <u>vingt-et-un</u> (16 + 5 = 21)
   c) trente − quinze = <u>quinze</u> (30 − 15 = 15)
   d) vingt-quatre − sept = <u>dix-sept</u> (24 − 7 = 17)
   e) vingt-huit − dix = <u>dix-huit</u> (28 − 10 = 18)
   f) dix-sept + huit = <u>vingt-cinq</u> (17 + 8 = 25)

3. Quel âge as-tu? — J'ai onze ans. — 11
   Quel âge ont-ils? — Ils ont seize ans. — 16
   Quel âge a-t-elle? — Elle a treize ans. — 13

   An Extra Challenge
   Henri a vingt ans.
   Maisam a huit ans.
   Sita a seize ans.

Pages 8-9 — Colours

1.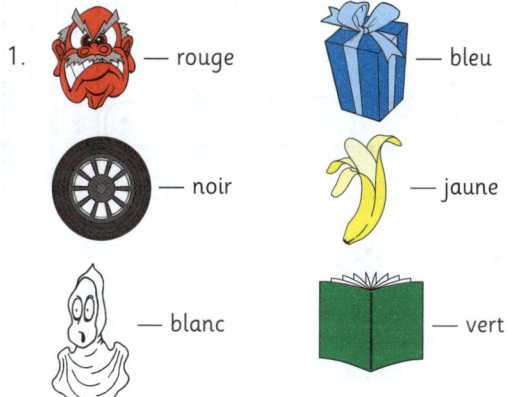
   — rouge
   — bleu
   — noir
   — jaune
   — blanc
   — vert

2. b) vert — green
   c) bleu — blue
   d) blanc — white
   e) rouge — red
   f) jaune — yellow

   An Extra Challenge
   le chapeau — Il est marron.
   la vache — Elle est rose.
   le chien — Il est violet.
   la fleur — Elle est orange.

35

Answers

Pages 10-11 — Months

1. a) avril
   b) septembre
   c) décembre
   d) juillet

2. C'est le deux juin.
   C'est le dix-huit septembre.
   C'est le vingt-six février.

3. b) It's the 30th of November.
   c) It's the 12th of July.
   d) It's the 4th of August.
   e) It's the 1st of April.

4. Any sensible answer, e.g.
   C'est le premier mai.

An Extra Challenge

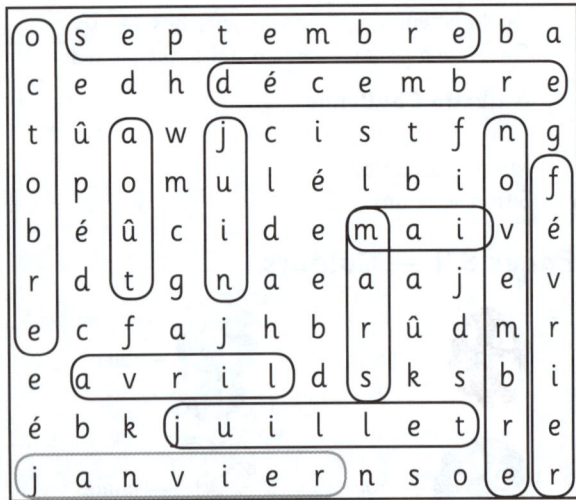

Pages 12-13 — My family

1. a) Tu as des frères ou des sœurs?
   b) Oui, j'ai deux sœurs et un frère.
   c) Je m'appelle Adam et je suis fils unique.

2. b) 20 years old
   c) Élodie's stepfather
   d) 15 years old
   e) Geoffrey
   f) Élodie's grandmother
   g) Emily

An Extra Challenge

Je m'appelle Ronan. J'ai un <u>frère</u> qui s'appelle Jaxon. <u>Ma mère</u> s'appelle Maya et <u>mon père</u> s'appelle Hamed. <u>Mon grand-père</u> s'appelle Derek et <u>ma grand-mère</u> s'appelle Pauline.
Any sensible answer, e.g. 'Je m'appelle Rachel. J'ai une sœur qui s'appelle Violet. Mon père s'appelle Kevin.'

Pages 14-15 — Animals

1. a) l'araignée
   b) le chien
   c) le poisson
   d) le serpent

2. a) la tortue
   b) le lapin
   c) l'oiseau
   d) le cheval

3. a) three
   b) False — Claude has three spiders.
   c) Claude's cat
   d) 2 years old
   e) rabbits

An Extra Challenge

Any sensible answer to the question 'As-tu un animal?', e.g.
J'ai deux hamsters. Les hamsters s'appellent Nibbles et Pickles. Ils ont deux ans.

Pages 16-17 — Clothes

1. a) trousers
   b) gloves
   c) shirt
   d) skirt
   e) dress
   f) jeans

2. b) Je porte des chaussures.
   c) Je porte des chaussettes.
   d) Je porte un pull.

3. You should have circled:
   Elle porte une jupe rose.
   Il porte un pantalon rouge.
   Elle porte une robe orange.

An Extra Challenge
a) Florian
b) black
c) Kalena
d) Florian
e) red

Answers

Pages 18-19 — Magical masters

1. You should have drawn:

2. a) horse = 5 points, white = 10 points.
      5 + 10 = <u>15</u> points.
   b) tortoise = 5 points, orange = 15 points.
      5 + 15 = <u>20</u> points.
   c) bird = 3 points, yellow = 12 points.
      3 + 12 = <u>15</u> points.
   d) fish = 7 points, red = 12 points.
      7 + 12 = <u>19</u> points.
   e) spider = 3 points, brown = 10 points.
      3 + 10 = <u>13</u> points.
   You should have circled b, the orange tortoise.

3. a) le fromage
      la pomme
      la pizza
      le yaourt
      le chocolat
   b) You should have circled: le fromage, le yaourt, le chocolat.
      You should have underlined: la pomme, la pizza.

4. J'aime jouer au foot. J'aime écouter de la musique à six heures du soir. Je n'aime pas regarder la télé. J'aime lire parce que c'est intéressant. Je n'aime pas jouer du piano parce que c'est ennuyeux.

Pages 20-21 — Food

1.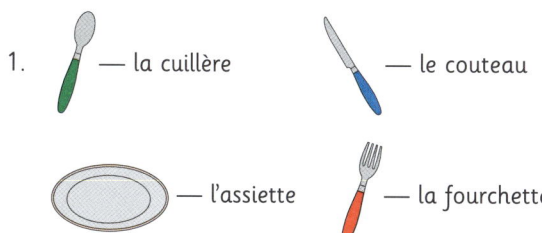

2. le fromage
   le jambon
   le yaourt

3. a) Can you pass me the fork, please?
   b) I'm eating (some) chocolate.
   c) Can you pass me the spoon?
   d) I would like a plate.

An Extra Challenge

 — Rowena

 — Gabe

Any sensible list, e.g. Je voudrais les spaghettis, deux pizzas et un sandwich.

Pages 22-23 — What do you like doing?

1. I like watching TV.
   I don't like dancing.
   I like playing football.

2. J'aime jouer du piano.
   J'aime écouter de la musique.
   Je n'aime pas nager.

3. a) reading and playing football
   b) playing football
   c) dancing
   d) watching TV
   e) reading

An Extra Challenge

Any sensible sentences about your hobbies, e.g. J'aime danser, parce que c'est fantastique. Je n'aime pas jouer du piano, parce que c'est ennuyeux.

Pages 24-25 — What time is it?

1. Il est huit heures et quart. —

   Il est onze heures et demie. —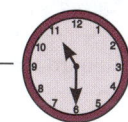

   Il est minuit. —

   Il est trois heures et demie. —

2. b) watch TV
   c) six o'clock in the evening
   d) listen to music

3. Il est cinq heures.
   Il est neuf heures.

Answers

4. Any sensible sentence about the time, e.g.
   Il est neuf heures et quart du matin.

   An Extra Challenge
   À trois heures, j'aime jouer au foot.
   À six heures et quart du soir, j'aime danser.
   Any sensible sentence about when you do your own hobbies, e.g.
   À cinq heures du soir j'aime lire.

Pages 26-27 — The weather

1. Il fait beau. — It's nice weather.
   Il fait froid — It's cold.
   Il neige. — It's snowing.
   Il fait chaud. — It's hot.
   Il fait mauvais. — It's bad weather.
2. Il y a du soleil.
   Il y a du vent.
   Il pleut.
   Il neige.
3. Any sensible sentence about the weather, e.g.
   Aujourd'hui il fait froid et il y a du soleil.
4. a) Il fait mauvais.
   b) Il fait froid.
   c) Il fait chaud.

   An Extra Challenge
   Any sensible sentences and pictures that complete the information in the diary, e.g.

Pages 28-29 — In my town

1. la poste
   la piscine
   le restaurant
2. a) no
   b) two
   c) one
   d) three
   e) yes

3. b) Opposite the restaurant.
   c) Next to the post office.

   An Extra Challenge
   Any sensible sentences about what is in your town and where places are, e.g.
   Dans ma ville, il y a deux cafés, une gare, un restaurant et des magasins. La gare est près du restaurant et en face du café.

Pages 30-31 — Masculine and feminine

1. a) <u>Mon</u> pull est violet.
   b) <u>Ma</u> jupe est rose.
      <u>Mon</u> t-shirt est jaune.
   c) <u>Mon</u> chien est marron et blanc. <u>Mon</u> chat est orange et violet.
   d) <u>Mon</u> chapeau est bleu et <u>ma</u> chemise est verte.
2. masculine: le chapeau, le fromage, le t-shirt
   feminine: la robe, la pizza, la souris, la tortue
3. Je porte <u>un</u> chapeau orange et <u>une</u> chemise rose.
   J'ai <u>un</u> frère et <u>une</u> sœur.
   Je mange <u>une</u> pomme, <u>un</u> yaourt et <u>un</u> sandwich.

   An Extra Challenge
   <u>Mon</u> frère s'appelle Johan et <u>ma</u> sœur s'appelle Femke.
   J'aime regarder <u>la</u> télé et écouter de <u>la</u> musique.
   Dans ma ville, il y a <u>une</u> piscine et <u>un</u> restaurant.

Page 32 — Plurals

1. b) mes hamsters
   c) des pommes
   d) les magasins
   e) des robes
   f) mes serpents
   g) les t-shirts
   h) mes pulls
2. a) She is wearing / wears (some) shoes.
   b) I eat / am eating (some) chips.
   c) My brothers are called Henri and Léo.